Dear Kone & Jeff —

We hope the pictures remind you of D pleasant visit to Bermuda.

Bill Shore.
Elbow Beach.
Oct. '97.

Published and distributed in Bermuda by:
Picturesque
The Design Centre, 129 Front Street
Hamilton HMCX, Bermuda

First Edition

10 9 8 7 6 5 4 3 2 1

ISBN 976-8157-04-6

Project Coordinated by:
Laura Herrmann Design
69 Atlantic Road
Gloucester, MA 01930

Editor
Shawna Mullen

Text
Tom & Onalee Cooke
with Bryan Darby

Design/Production
Laura Herrmann

Printed and bound in Hong Kong
Paramount Printing Co. Ltd.

(right) Fordham Hall, Pembroke

PICTURESQUE BERMUDA

Photographs by Roland Skinner

CONTENTS

(left) Hamilton Harbour

PREFACE

While working on this book, I suddenly realized how fortunate I am to have been born on this picturesque island, and to be able to appreciate the incredible beauty that surrounds me. After all these years, the anticipation of waiting for the film to be processed still excites me.

Our seasons provide a variety of lighting opportunities. I particularly like winter, when the sun's lower trajectory provides lovely shadows all day long. This is also the best time to photograph the beaches, with natural patterns in the sand carved by wind and tide. Light and shadow plays a very important role in photography. At some point in every day, the light will show the subject at its best. The key is to capture the image at this time. Two of my favorite times to photograph are the "golden hours", which are the first and last hours of the day, and those moments when the distant sky turns grey and the subject is still brightly lit by the sun.

Bermuda's small size is a further advantage. Being familiar with the island's wind directions, lighting and tides, I am able to determine the best time and location to capture an image.

I hope you enjoy the images in this book as much as I have enjoyed photographing them.

(left) Stamp House, Warwick

Roland Skinner

BERMUDA

The island chain of Bermuda lies some 700 miles off the coast of the United States, a thousand miles north of the Caribbean and some 3,000 miles south-east of Great Britain. This strategic location in the middle of the Atlantic has ensured Bermuda a role in every man-made endeavour of the past five hundred years, from armed conflict to maritime development, to the evolution of tourism and international business.

The natural beauty of the 22-square-mile chain of inter-connected islands owes its genesis to a rare volcanic eruption millions of years ago that thrust a pillar of molten lava up from the seabed to the surface some 13,000 feet above. In due course, the benign climate created by the nearby Gulf Stream helped make a cap of coral on top of the lava and limestone cliffs appeared above the sea. Rich soil blown from the African continent fell providentially to a depth of three feet on the bare rock, and nature assumed its responsibility, adding birds, fish, and foliage until a paradise had been created.

The first humans to discover Bermuda were Spanish and Portuguese explorers, including Juan de Bermudez whose visit in the 1500s gave the tiny archipelago its name. The earliest maps of the area show Bermuda as a navigation mark for the fleets of the Spanish Main, who, once they had sighted the islands, turned right for the Old World.

It took the British and quite different circumstances to establish the full-time occupation of Bermuda. Caught in a fierce hurricane in the summer of 1609, the flagship of a fleet of British ships chartered by settlers on their way to Virginia was shipwrecked on the Bermuda reef to the point of sinking.

With its abundant fish, birds, hogs, and cedar forests, the island chain offered the British an intriguing prize; by 1612 it had been claimed for the Crown and by 1620 it had been settled and given its own parliament. It remains to this day one of the oldest democracies in the Western World.

The people of Bermuda represent a wide cross-section of nationalities, many being descended from British adventurers, African slaves, Caribbean seafarers, Indian tribes, Portuguese farmers, American traders, and Canadian mariners. The emancipation of the slaves was accomplished in Bermuda ahead of most other communities and the franchise expanded in due course to include both races.

The isolated position of Bermuda demanded an industrious population from the first days of colonization, and historians record that the islanders tried every imaginable means of making a living, from pearl fishing to tobacco growing, from farming to ship-building. Fortunately, when one door closed another always seemed to open for the enterprising islanders.

The expulsion of the British from America in the late 1700s was a case in point. This led directly to the creation of a fortified dockyard for the British Navy, a mammoth undertaking that saw 9,000 convicts labour for 40 years to transform a 214-acre stretch of barren islands into the "Gibraltar of the West".

The strategic position of Bermuda was to come into its own over the intervening 200 years, as global conflict made its presence an essential ingredient — with British, American, and Canadian bases being established over ten percent of its tiny land mass.

True to their industrious leanings, the Bermudians were among the first to appreciate the economic benefits of tourism and for over a century now the island has held onto the reputation of being a quality vacation destination. With the development of hotels and the cruise ship industry carefully controlled by the elected Government, Bermuda reigned supreme throughout the first half of this century as a leader in the field of hospitality.

Now that competition is worldwide and the need to diversify becoming more urgent, the people of Bermuda have cleverly added the arrow of international business to their quiver, in the sure knowledge that the first-class hotels, restaurants, golf courses, and beaches are just as much a lure to the businessman as they are to the tourist. As a result, the island's billion-dollar GDP is shared equally now by the two industries, and the envied lifestyle of the average Bermudian continues to be among the highest in the world.

The population of Bermuda is around 58,000 — with a ratio of sixty percent black to forty percent white. The island is a Dependent Territory of the United Kingdom and a recent referendum on independence produced a vote in favour of retaining the status quo. Its parliament, which has an elected lower house of 40 seats and an appointed Senate with 11 seats, follows the Westminster system and is presided over by a Governor selected by Her Majesty the Queen.

The emergence of a beautiful tourist destination as one of the world's leading insurance centres, and the fact that its financial institutions are now recognized as industry leaders around the globe, gives further indication of the ability of this small community to make an impact far beyond its physical dimensions.

As it heads towards the next millennium and its 400th birthday, the unique Bermuda society that was created out of rugged individualism over the centuries can be forgiven the motto *Quo Fata Ferunt*, which translates into "Whither the Fates May Lead."

Bryan Darby

SHORELINE

erpetual breezes whet the appetite of the sportsman who enjoys wind surfing and sailing. The crystalline quality of the water attracts fishermen, snorklers, and scuba divers alike. The fascination of the reefs lures anglers from boats, cliff tops, or the shore. A climb along the rocks leads to discovery: one can look into the shallow pools and spot a rainbow-hued parrot fish lazily feeding on the coral. The South Shore is a study in

Spittal Pond
Nature Reserve

contrasts — from its smooth pink necklace of beaches, to its steep cliffs (home of the graceful longtail). There you may also find oddly shaped pinnacles, whose craggy surfaces have been eroded by the prevailing southern waves until they resemble a strange, lunar landscape. Winds and tides have masterfully etched arches and dramatic rock formations, such as those found at Natural Arches near Tucker's Town in the east and at Cathedral Rocks in Ely's Harbour in the west. On the North Shore, where the water is better protected by the coral reef, the shoreline has a gentler appearance. The island does have its inshore waters as well, and here the shoreline is more civilized, with natural harbours offering wonderful waterfront locations and protected moorings for boats.

Gurnet Rock
off Castle Roads

South Shore
Rocks and Surf

Robinson's Bay
Devonshire

Castle Island
Castle Harbour

Dingles Island
Harrington Sound

Dingles Bay
Harrington Sound

Building Shell
Smith's Parish

Riddells Bay

Bermuda
Fitted Dinghies

Spittal Pond
Shoreline

Tide at Flatts Inlet
Smith's Parish

Netting Bait

Devonshire Bay

COUNTRYSIDE

*A*long the lanes and byways of Bermuda, royal palms stand in stately procession among a profusion of flowering vegetation. Walls lining the roads give the byways a special character and the adjacent landscape a pastoral coziness. Often, roads thread through limestone banks that have been cut away, leaving behind a natural wall. Here and there, walls end in a flourish with a white pillar decoratively topped with a small pyramid-shape. Farms bordered by weathered

stone walls dot hillsides where cows, chickens, and goats graze contentedly. Freshly plowed fields of russet-red soil sleepily await the first green shoots to appear in their neat rows. Hedges and arches of oleander create romantic bowers of cheerful pink blossoms along the lanes. Verdant lawns, sprinkled with

Paget Marsh (left)

Southampton
Shoreline (above)

wild, starry-petaled freesias in springtime, hint of secret gardens beyond. Roadside stands sell produce from carefully tended farmers' gardens. On the old railway paths, walkers find peace and solitude, or are mesmerized by a lovely cove that seems to appear out of nowhere. Suddenly the tranquillity is shattered by the strident call of the kiskadee, a cheeky, yellow-breasted bird.

Botanical Gardens

Moongate

Farmlands
Devonshire

Farmlands
Smith's Parish

Entrance to Southlands
Warwick

Morning Mist
Devonshire Marsh

Railway Trail
Somerset

Clockwise from top left: Riddells Bay Golf Course, Belmont Golf Course, Southampton Princess Golf Course,
Mid Ocean Golf Course, Ocean View Golf Course, Castle Harbour Golf Course

St. George's Golf Course, Port Royal Golf Course

SAND & SEA

Nonsuch Island
(left)

Warwick Long Bay
(above)

Nowhere in Bermuda is more than a mile from the shore, so it stands to reason that the sea plays an important part in the lives of the island's inhabitants. Because of the protective barrier reef that surrounds the 22-square-miles of land, much of the fury of the unforgiving Atlantic is muted, and as a consequence the shoreline is an unforgettable delight. Water so clear that you can see waving coral fronds a hundred yards away is just one feature that tempts the writer to bring out his pen, and the photographer his lens. Look at the sand. It isn't even humble enough to be traditional white or gold. It's pink! Tiny pieces of shell, ground-up red coral, pumice stone, and limestone can be found in the pink Bermuda beaches that dot the shoreline, like the crescent-shaped bites of an ancient sea god who thought Bermuda looked good enough to eat. There is food there, of course, in the shape of lobsters, conch, pompano, rockfish, and snapper — but the real thrill is to walk on the beach at any time of the day or night and enjoy the sand underfoot, the sea breeze in one's hair, and the scent of sargasso seaweed caught in a tidal rock pool.

Jobson's Cove
Warwick

Sand & Sea

Natural Arches
Tucker's Town

Stonehole Bay
Warwick

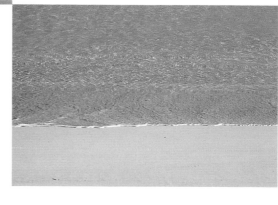

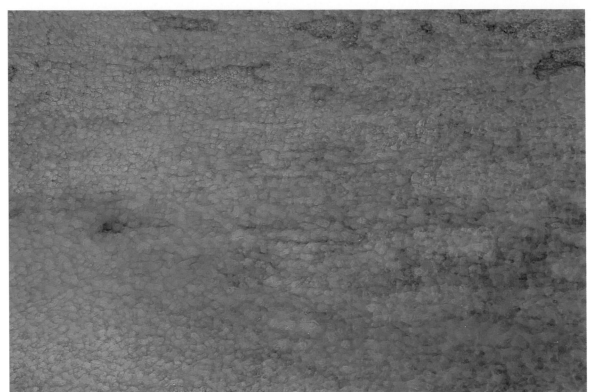

Grape Bay

Horseshoe Bay

Whale Bay
Southampton

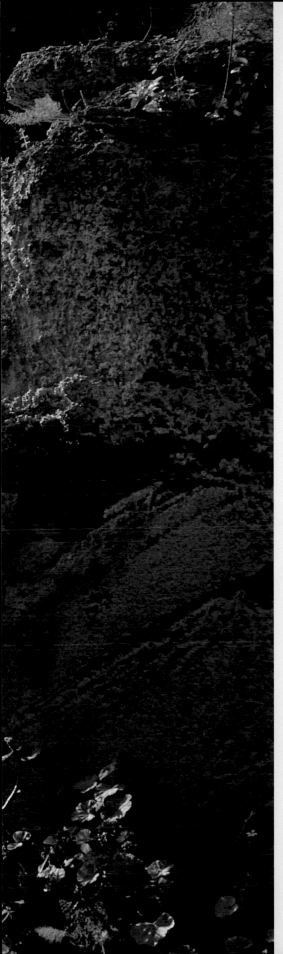

FLORA

Easter Lily
Lilium longiflorum

he romance and charm of these sun-drenched isles is created by abundant flowers amidst lush greenery. Colour startles and excites at every turn. Fluorescent hues seem at home in this semi-tropical climate, and bloom in a dazzling floral spectrum — hibiscus hedges in tints from soft pink to brilliant orange, waterfalls of fuchsia bougainvillaea, pink avenues of lacy oleander, royal poinciana trees spreading graceful branches of bright red-orange clusters, and the tiny, indigenous bermudiana, peeking up as sweetly as bright blue stars in the grass. The simplicity of rampant orange, red, and yellow nasturtiums that join purple-blue morning glories to blanket pathways and embankments; the elegance of a field of pure white Easter lilies; the mystery of the tangled root systems and shaded taupes of banyan and Indian rubber trees; and everywhere, yellow fountains of golden shower trees, sunny yellow allamandas twining over trellises and porticos, and shiny spice tree leaves scenting the air with cinnamon and clove.

Oleander
Nerium oleander

Madagascar Periwinkle
Catharanthus roseus

Coralita
Antigonon leptopus

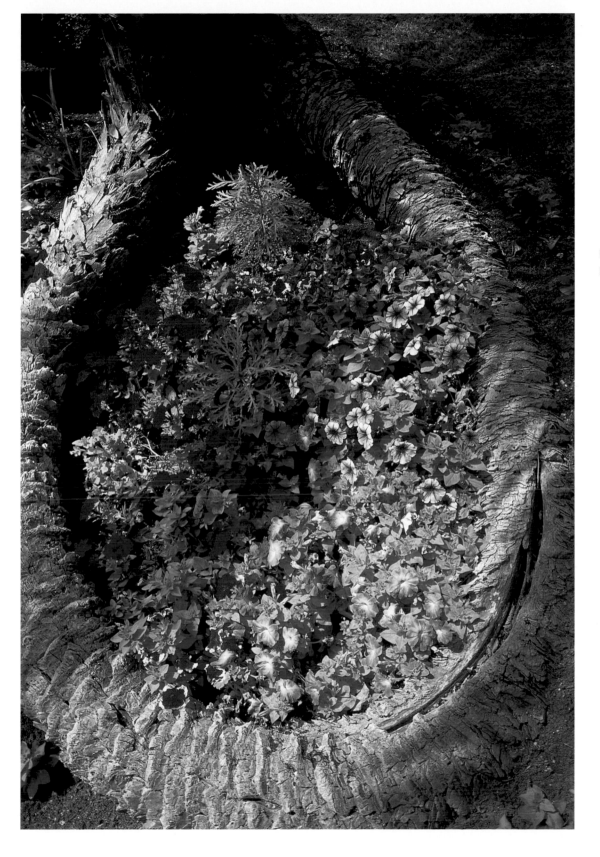

Petunia
Petunia x hybrida

Pigeon Berry
Duranta repens

Royal Poinciana
Delonix regia

Golden Shower
Cassia fistula

Clockwise from top left: Bird of Paradise, Hibiscus, Giant Bird of Paradise,
Night Blooming Cereus, Rose, Mexican Sunflower

Clockwise from top left: Calla Lily, Waterlily, Petunia,
Freesia, Canna Lily, Nasturtium

Yellow Allamanda
Allamanda cathartica

Cat's Claw Vine
Macfadyena unguis-cati

Oleander
Nerium oleander

Spanish Bayonet
Yucca aloifolia

Pampas Grass
Cortaderia selloana

Bay Grape
Coccoloba uvifera

Surinam Cherry
Eugenia uniflora

Loquat
Eriobotrya japonica

Morning Glory
Ipomoea purpurea

Ruellia

Bermudiana
Sisyrinchium bermudians

FROM ABOVE

When viewed from above, whether in a helicopter or from a perch atop Gibbs Hill lighthouse, the appearance of these isles changes dramatically. Your first impression is how isolated Bermuda seems, sitting totally alone in the middle of the Atlantic. But in the space of a thought, you are struck by her startling beauty: the lushness of the land itself, quite emerald in its brilliance. The colour of the water — so intensely turquoise it seems tinted by some giant inkwell

View from West
(left)

View from East
(above)

that has spilled — washes crystal clear in the shallows, then transforms from aqua to cobalt to almost navy blue at the horizon. The water is so clear that boats, gathering in great numbers in coves, bays, and small harbours, seem to be sitting on the very bottom of the ocean floor. Intersecting reefs create stars and fascinating designs. From a lofty vantage point, golf courses become shocking-green, abstract shapes, while hedgerows and walls join verdant farmlands and byways into a neat patchwork quilt. Tractors plowing sienna-red dirt sketch patterns as they crisscross the landscape. The result is a scene of surreal beauty, as dazzling as any spectacle on earth.

Castle Roads
Tucker's Town

Castle Island, Charles Island, Fricks Point

From Above

St. David's Island

The Causeway
St. George's

Jobson's Cove

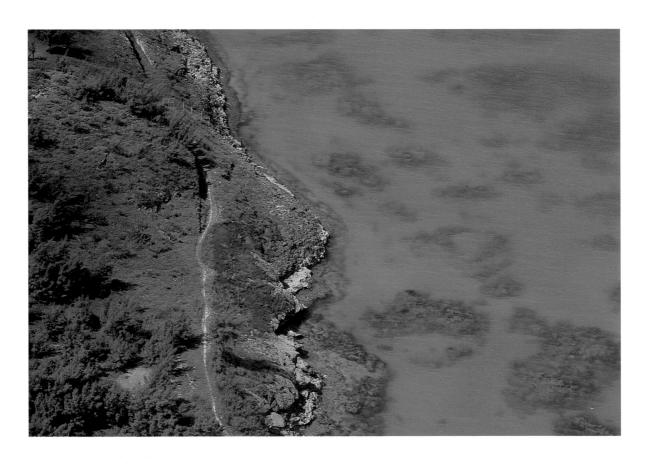

Railway Trail

Coral Reefs

Lighthouse View

Gibbs Hill Lighthouse
Southampton

Fishermen
Netting Bait

Nonsuch Island

From Above

St. George's

Town Cut
St. George's

ARCHITECTURE

Much of the enchantment and visual allure of Bermuda lies in its imaginative style of architecture, surely like nothing else in the world. Driven by the ravages of hurricanes, the early settlers designed sturdy limestone houses with overlapping slate roofs that would have delighted even the most demanding architect. Pretty as they may be, the important thing about these houses is that they have stood the test of time and tempest. And so, in the manner of

dwellings all over the world, the basic Bermuda home became a symbol of wealth and social status, and the experimentation began. Scalloped gables echo the style of Portuguese artisans, graceful arches reflect a Moorish influence, moongates speak of voyages to the Far East. But there are Bermudian influences, too: The decorative "eyebrow" cornices over windows, which give a personality to each home, and the unusual "welcoming arms" stairways that gently beckon the visitor to enter. And the colours, the colours! The pastel cottages look like a cluster of paintbox splashes — pink, orange, blue, green, and yes, even lavender. Anywhere else the combination would be decidedly bizarre, but in Bermuda, it all seems a most harmonious blend.

Springfield
Somerset

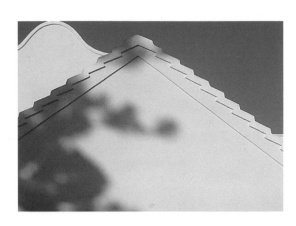

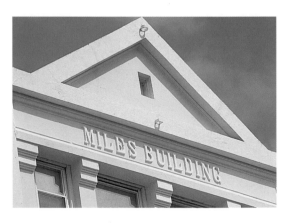
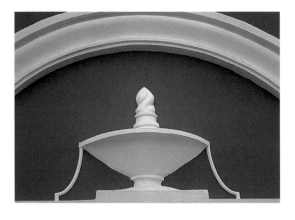

MILES BUILDING

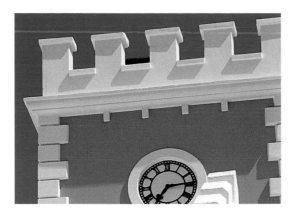

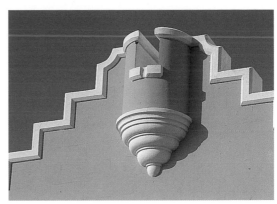

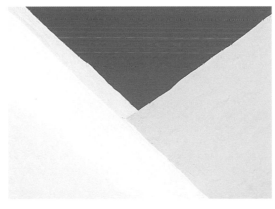

Carter House
St. David's Island

Heydon Trust Chapel

Pembroke Rectory

Pembroke Rectory

Railway Trail View

Old Chimney
Shelly Bay

SKYLINE

The end of a beautiful day is really just the beginning. Pink- and blue-tinged clouds are reflected in the smooth, wet sand and tidal pools along the beach. Bermuda sunsets, as well as sunrises, awaken your senses as Mother Nature tries to compete with the rainbow-hued cottages. Longtails glide toward their evening nests in the rocky cliffs. A late evening breeze sets off restless rattling in the palm trees, whose silhouettes are dark against a glowing orange sky dappled with purple clouds.

Foot of the Lane

Returning to Hamilton on the end-of-day ferry from Dockyard, one gasps at the beauty of cloud formations clustered over the land. On one side, Gibbs Hill lighthouse, its reassuring beacon scanning the sky; on the other, the city of Hamilton, its twinkling lights reflected in the harbour. Soon the sky deepens to navy, and diamond stars appear. Tree frogs begin their evening serenade and land crabs scuttle sideways across the lanes and byways. The intoxicating scent of frangipani and citrus blossoms perfumes the evening air.

Feathered Clouds

Lighthouse View
Riddells Bay

Old Man in the Boat

Skyline

Moongate
Shelly Bay

Watford Bridge
Somerset

Longtail

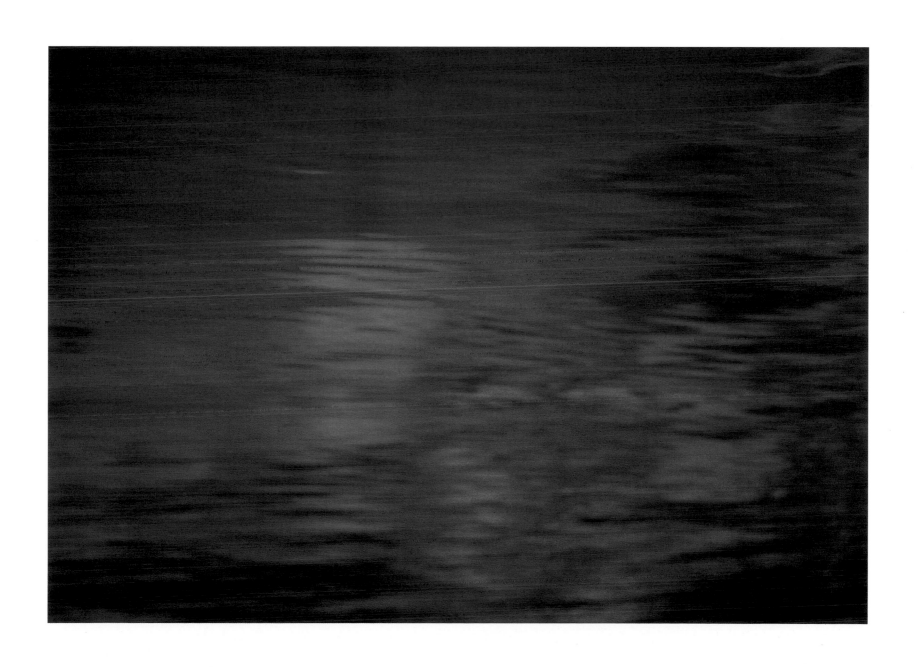